C000144391

Absolutely basic

Absolutely basic

An updated and shortened version of
'The Everlasting Righteousness'
by Horatius Bonar (1808-1889)

together with

an updated and shortened version of three sermons on
'Regeneration'
from 'The Christian Race and other Sermons'
by J. C. Ryle (1816-1900)

GRACE PUBLICATIONS TRUST
7 Arlington Way
London EC1R 1XA
England
e-mail: AGBCSE@aol.com
www.gracepublications.co.uk

Managing Editors: T. I. Curnow and M. J. Adams

© Grace Publications Trust

First published 2009
ISBN 978-0-94646-279-7
ISBN 0-94646-279-8

Unless otherwise indicated Scripture quotations are taken from the HOLY BIBLE, NEW INTERNATIONAL VERSION. Copyright © 1973, 1978, 1984 by International Bible Society. Used by permission of Hodder & Stoughton, a member of the Hodder Headline Group. All rights reserved.

Scripture quotations marked (ESV) are from the Holy Bible, English Standard Version, published by HarperCollins Publishers © 2001 by Crossway Bibles, a division of Good News Publishers. Used by permission. All rights reserved.

Scripture quotations marked (NASV) are taken from the NEW AMERICAN STANDARD BIBLE®, Copyright © 1960,1962,1963,1968,1971,1972,19 73,1975,1977,1995 by The Lockman Foundation. Used by permission.

Distributed by
EP BOOKS
Faverdale North
Darlington DL3 OPH
England

e-mail: sales@epbooks.org
www.epbooks.org

Cover design by Lawrence Evans

Printed and bound in UK by the MPG Books Group

Contents

Part One

Righteous for ever

A shortened version of 'The Everlasting Righteousness' by
Horatius Bonar, first published in 1874.
The full work is available from the Banner of Truth Trust.

Prepared by Ruth Firth

Introduction

About the author

Horatius Bonar (1808-1889) was a minister in Scotland for over 50 years. He was a very modest man, and did not want anyone to write about him after his death; during his lifetime he wrote many tracts and books, but is best known today as the writer of many great hymns, including *I hear the words of love* and *Thy works, not mine, O Christ*.

About the book

His book *The Everlasting Righteousness* was first published in 1874.

Its central theme is the substitutionary work of Jesus Christ. Bonar shows that, in Jesus Christ, God has provided the only way to deal with the problem of our sin. Jesus lived a life of perfect obedience to God, and completely satisfied all the demands of God's holy law. He then died the death that sinners deserve.

Because Jesus is the perfect substitute, anyone who believes in him receives a legal pardon from God, and the perfect righteousness of Jesus becomes theirs.

This truth has enormous consequences for believers, and Bonar explains some of them in this wonderful book.

God has used this book as a great blessing in my life, and it is my hope that this simplified version will help you, the reader, to understand more of what Jesus has done for you, so that he will become more precious to you.

Ruth Firth
March 2009

Chapter 1
Understanding our problem

There is one great question that every person asks at some time or other: 'How can I, a sinner, come to God, who is perfect, and not be afraid of punishment?' People have tried to find answers to this question, but it is no surprise that no one has come close to answering it. We don't really even understand the question we are asking, because we don't really understand what sin is, that sin is actually guilt, for which God will judge us.

People consistently treat sin as if it were an unfortunate event, not a crime; or as some kind of disease, not as guilt. It's as if we think we need a doctor to solve the problem of sin, when actually we need a judge. This is where we go wrong; sin is *guilt* and must be punished. The guilt of the offender (that is, the sinner) must be dealt with before we can answer the question of how a sinful human being can have a relationship with a perfect God.

If we look at human history we ought to be able to see very clearly that sin is a crime, which God hates and must punish. Sin is serious, and has serious consequences — or how else can we explain thousands of graveyards, where loved ones are buried? Is death just 'natural'? Or what about millions of broken-hearted people — is that 'just the way life is'? Or the casualties of war — can we look at such things and still maintain that human beings are essentially good? Or look at earthquakes, hurricanes, volcanoes — don't these also show us the consequences of sin? Or our own emptiness, pain, depression — don't all these clearly point to one thing: that sin is *guilt*, and must be punished? If we don't admit this, then we are actually defending the idea that moral confusion and injustice are normal.

Despite all this, the human race as a whole refuses to see sin as evil, and instead tries to explain it away as a momentary lapse from which we will soon recover. We try to deal with our sin ourselves, and by doing this we only make our situation worse! All our efforts to get rid of our sin in fact just add to it, and if we try to come to God without first admitting our guilt, we only make ourselves more guilty! Sin is far too evil for us to handle ourselves. Once we see this, we have to acknowledge that only God can deal with sin.

So we have seen that in trying to answer this question we must properly understand the seriousness of sin. We must also understand more clearly who God is. We like to think of God as a loving Father, and he is. But he is also a righteous Judge. Can he stop being a Judge, and only be a Father? Or the other way round? Yes, God loves sinners, but he also hates their sin. Should he stop loving sinners because he hates sin, or stop hating sin because he loves sinners? God has said that he doesn't enjoy it when sinners die (Ezek. 33:11), but he has also said that everyone who sins will die (Ezek. 18:4). Which of these does he mean? Or can he mean them both? In order for sinners to have a relationship with God, his love (God as Father) and his law (God as Judge) must somehow be able to peacefully co-exist. People have tried to reconcile

God's law and God's love, but their attempts have always failed, because they always end up making God's love more important than God's law, when actually both are equally important.

Can I come close to God, and not die? Can I come into the presence of a God who hates sin, and yet find that the sin he hates does not prevent me from coming to him? Can my worship of God be accepted by him? God has the answer to all these questions, and that answer is found in his court of law. God comes into his court, bringing his case against sinful people, and he himself provides a way to legally resolve the case, in such a way that his justice is satisfied, and man is found not guilty.

As we have said, only God can deal with sin. He does so legally, so that any sinner on earth can come into God's court and have the problem of his sin dealt with. All that is needed is for the guilty person to agree to accept God's solution, and he is declared innocent. He then leaves the court with a clear conscience, free of guilt. He is at peace with God, and God is at peace with him.

God's solution shows how sinful our sin is, and how perfect God's law is, yet at the same time it means that God can love sinful people without bending or breaking his law. God has reconciled his love and his law, without either of them giving way to the other. In fact, both God's love and his law have been displayed completely, in all their beauty, and both of them have been completely satisfied.

Romans 3:20 says, 'Through the law we become conscious of sin.' Sin and law are connected, and this connection must be kept, both in punishing sin and in forgiving sin. God's law, like God himself, cannot change, so both the punishment and the forgiveness of sin must be carried out in a way that keeps God's law. God has made a way so that his law can be perfectly kept, and yet at the same time sinners can be legally forgiven. He has worked things out so that his law, which once rightly accused us of being guilty, now rightly defends us as being innocent. How he has done this we will see in the next chapter.

Chapter 2
God's solution — substitution

In chapter 1 we saw that only God can deal with man's sin, and that he does so by a legal process. This process is called substitution: someone who is innocent takes the place of someone who is guilty, and is punished instead of them.

The only time that this is allowed in a human court of law is when a person owes money. In that case, his debt can be paid by someone else. Then the person who was owed the money is satisfied, and there is no need for a trial, even though the debtor has not paid the money back personally.

For all other cases of breaking the law, however, the guilty person himself has to be punished in order for justice to be done. But God does not deal with our guilt in that way. He uses substitution (someone else being punished) to deal with all our breaking of his law. We can't completely understand how substitution works, but it is how God has decided to deal with our sin.

We see this principle of substitution being used throughout the Bible, beginning with Adam and Eve. After they sinned God gave them a promise — that Eve's descendant would crush the serpent's head, and that the serpent would strike this descendant's heel (Gen. 3:15). This promise means that Jesus would defeat Satan by allowing Satan to strike him. The fact that God replaced the clothes which Adam and Eve had made out of fig leaves using animal skins instead — which meant that the animal had to die — also shows us something of the idea of substitution, and that it was the way in which God intended to deal with sinful people.

Then we have Cain and Abel. God accepts Abel's sacrifice, and rejects Cain's (Gen. 4:3-5). Why? Because Abel offered a lamb, and God accepted the death of that animal in Abel's place, as a temporary substitute, until Jesus would come — the descendant of Eve promised in Genesis 3:15. Cain's sacrifice, and so Cain himself, was rejected because his sacrifice did not involve the death of a substitute.

So we see that right from the beginning God dealt with people on the basis of the innocent dying for the guilty. All the major figures in the Old Testament — Noah, Abraham, Isaac, Jacob — brought sacrifices like Abel's. They understood (although not in every detail) that these sacrifices pointed to Jesus — the One who could take the punishment for their guilt and survive it, when they could not.

In the Passover (Exod. 12) the lamb's blood protected the people from death. Inside the house people might have worried, wondering how some blood on the doorpost could keep them safe from the destroyer. But no amount of worrying could change the fact that the lamb's blood was on the doorpost, and that God would see it. So they were safe, and could eat the Passover meal with thankfulness and joy.

After their escape from Egypt, while they were still in the desert, God gave them a more detailed system of sacrifices. Up to this point there had only been one kind of sacrifice, but now this was split up into many different parts. The main reason for this was to show God's people how completely the principle of substitution dealt with their guilt and brought them forgiveness, cleansing, acceptance and blessing.

To summarise, this is what the system of sacrifices has to teach us:

1. God is angry at sin, and must punish it.
2. The sinner offers a substitute in place of himself.
3. God's anger is directed towards the substitute, instead of the sinner.
4. The substitute is killed in place of the sinner.
5. God views the sinner as being as perfect as the substitute he offered.
6. The sinner is at peace with God, accepted completely by him, and enjoys his approval and love.

Substitution is God's way of making sinners acceptable to him, so that they can approach him confidently, with a clean conscience (Heb. 9:14). God's holiness is satisfied as he looks at the perfect substitute, Jesus Christ. He says, 'That sacrifice is enough for me.' So then sinners can also look at the same substitute, agree with God and say, 'It's enough for me, too.' This is at the centre of the gospel. We believe and declare that God freely loves sinners — that's the first part of the message. The second part is how God has righteously made this love available to sinners. The gospel is all about who God is, and what Jesus Christ has done. Anyone who believes it has eternal life (Acts 13:39).

A sinner might bring his sacrifice with weak faith and a fearful heart. But his salvation doesn't depend on the strength of his faith, but on whether the sacrifice is perfect or not. The weakest faith can read the words 'The blood of Jesus, his Son, purifies us from all sin' (1 John 1:7), and even if there may be times when we wonder if this is really true, those words are still there; our doubting doesn't make them disappear. God says that the person who believes is declared innocent — so who are we to question God's word?

Some people spend a lot of time worrying about whether they really believe or not; so much so, that they sideline Jesus' work. They don't think so much about what Jesus has done as they do about what they have to do to get connected to him. This is actually being self-righteous. Imagine that an Israelite comes to the temple with his lamb, and then spends a long time debating with himself about the right way of putting his hands on the lamb's head. Then after he offers the sacrifice, he goes away worrying about whether or not he put his hands in the right place or pressed hard enough on the lamb's head. Wouldn't you want to remind him that the lamb was the important thing, and that however much his hands were shaking, or however lightly or briefly they touched the lamb, that was enough? Touching the lamb just showed that he wanted God to take that lamb as his substitute. So the real question to worry about isn't 'Did I touch the lamb in the right way?', but 'Did I touch the right lamb — one that God will accept?' The most important question for the sinner isn't 'Do I have the right kind or the right amount of faith?', but 'Do I have *any* faith in Jesus?' He or she needs to know that Jesus died and was buried, and rose again. Knowing this is eternal life.

Chapter 3
Jesus the complete substitute

Jesus Christ came into the world to be a substitute for sinners; he not only died for sinners, but he also lived a perfect life for sinners. This perfect life and death of Jesus belongs to everyone who believes in him, and it is enough to cover all their sin, without exception.

The name 'Jesus' (meaning Saviour, Matt. 1:21) was given to him at his birth. This name made clear that his mission was to save sinners, and the fact that this name was given to him at the beginning of his life means that his whole life was part of this mission. His life's work was to save sinners, not just his death on the cross, and this meant that he was the sinners' substitute throughout his life, and not only on the cross.

Jesus began his life on earth in poverty, and as an outcast. Luke 2:7 tells us that there was no room for him in the inn. He was not even given a bed to sleep in, or a roof over his head; right from the beginning of his life until its end he was not welcomed, but treated as an outcast. 2 Corinthians 8:9 explains this: 'Though he was rich, yet for your sakes he became poor.' The circumstances of his birth show us that even at the beginning of his life Jesus was living for sinners. He was experiencing the rejection that sinners deserve.

After eight days he was circumcised. Circumcision was a sign that the person being circumcised was a sinner, and needed cleansing. We know that Jesus himself was holy, and without sin (Luke 1:35). The fact that he was circumcised means that he was not undergoing the ritual for himself, but as our substitute.

Circumcision was also a sign that the person submitted themselves to God's law. As Paul states in Galatians 5:3: 'I declare to every man who lets himself be circumcised that he is required to obey the whole law.' By being circumcised, Jesus was putting himself under an obligation to keep God's law — not for himself, because he was perfect, but for others. He was beginning a life of complete obedience to God's law on our behalf, as we read in Romans 5:19: 'For just as through the disobedience of the one man [Adam] the many were made sinners, so also through the obedience of the one man [Jesus] the many will be made righteous.'

We can only really understand why Jesus was baptised if we look at it in terms of substitution. Baptism symbolises death to and cleansing from sin. But Jesus was completely free from sin, so why would he be baptised, unless it was another sign that he was representing sinners? At his baptism Jesus said that he did it 'to fulfil all righteousness' (Matt. 3:15). His baptism was another part of his life as our substitute. He was being treated as if he were a sinner, so that he could stand in the place of sinners, and obey God perfectly instead of us, as we should have done.

In the book of Psalms we find Jesus expressing his feelings while bearing sins on the cross — sins which were not his own personally, but which he felt, just as if they were his own. For example in Psalm 22 we read these words: 'Many bulls surround me; strong bulls of Bashan encircle me … Dogs have surrounded me; a band of evil men has encircled me, they have pierced my hands and my feet' (Ps. 22: 12,16). Why did Jesus go through this experience? Because he was our substitute, who had taken our place, and undertaken to fight our enemies for us.

Jesus does not only express what he suffered on the cross while bearing our sins, but also what he suffered during his life on earth. An example of this is in Psalm 88:15: 'From my youth I have been afflicted and close to death; I have suffered your terrors and am in despair.' In verse 3 of the same Psalm he says, 'My soul is full of trouble and my life draws near the grave.' These are almost exactly the same words he uses in the Garden of Gethsemane: 'My soul is overwhelmed with sorrow to the point of death' (Matt. 26:38).

Again in Psalm 88:7-9 we read, 'Your wrath lies heavily upon me; you have overwhelmed me… You have taken from me my closest friends.' This is what Isaiah meant when he wrote about Jesus as 'despised and rejected by men, a man of sorrows, and familiar with suffering' (Isaiah 53:3). There can be no doubt that Jesus suffered all these things because he was carrying our sins all the way to the cross, as well as bearing them on the cross. Isaiah 53:4: 'Surely he took up our infirmities and carried our sorrows' is quoted in the New Testament (Matt. 8:17), referring to Jesus' daily ministry of healing. Jesus acted as our substitute from the moment of his birth, and when he said on the cross 'It is finished', in this he included his whole lifetime of bearing sins that were not his own.

Of course it is at the cross that we see most clearly Jesus acting as our substitute. It was at the cross that Jesus felt the full weight of our sin, and the full expression of God's anger against that sin. There he paid the full price for our sin — his life. And it is because of the cross that we are declared righteous and reconciled to God. The place of Jesus' death becomes the place of life for us.

The moment I believe, God credits me with Jesus' righteousness; I don't need to do anything. God is willing to receive me on the basis of Jesus' perfection, and if I am willing to be received that way, the deal is done. I am now represented by Jesus, and he appears for me in God's presence (Heb. 9:24). Everything that makes Jesus precious and dear to the Father has been transferred to me. Jesus' excellence and glory are seen as if they were mine, and I receive God's love, God's friendship and God's praise as if I had earned it all. I am so united to Jesus, my substitute, that God doesn't only treat me as if I hadn't done all the evil I have done, but as if I had done all the good that Jesus has done!

In one sense I am still a poor sinner, but in another sense I am also completely righteous, and will be for ever, because of Jesus, who is perfect for ever. It is in his perfection that I stand before God. This is not only true in theory, but in fact. I receive real blessings as a result — and so does any sinner who comes to trust in Jesus.

Chapter 4
A substitution that completely satisfies God

In the book of Isaiah, chapter 53, we have a prophecy about the cross. Up to this time the Israelites could understand some things about Jesus from the system of sacrifices God had given them, but in Isaiah 53 we are given much more detail about what Jesus came to do. God shows us more about the sinner's guilt being transferred to his substitute, and more about the love of God for sinful people. The theme of Isaiah 53 is the righteous One suffering for unrighteous people.

Let's look through this chapter to see what we can learn about Jesus. In verse 2 Jesus is described as growing up 'like a root out of dry ground' — this world, into which Jesus was born, was a hard environment, against him from the start. Jesus grew up amongst us, but he was not loved or admired or respected. Verse 3 says, 'he was despised and rejected by men', just like John says in his Gospel: 'He came to his own, and his own people did not receive him' (John 1:11, ESV).

Verse 3 continues by telling us that he was 'a man of sorrows, and familiar with suffering'. When angels are sent by God to the earth they do not experience sadness and suffering; they see the condition of the human race, and they do what God has sent them to do, but they are not personally affected. How can we explain the fact that Jesus was affected by this sinful world in a way that angels are not? It was because he was living as our Substitute, identifying himself with sinners, and therefore was sensitive to the effects of sin, and consciously experienced sadness and suffering. 'Surely he took up our infirmities and carried our sorrows' (verse 4). Jesus was a man of sorrows because he was carrying *our* sorrows. People could not understand this, and decided that God must be punishing Jesus for some sin of his own — this is what we read in the second half of verse 4: 'we considered him stricken by God, smitten by him, and afflicted.'

In verse 5 we have the real reason why Jesus was punished: 'He was pierced for *our* transgressions, he was crushed for *our* iniquities; the punishment that brought *us* peace was upon him, and by his wounds *we* are healed.' The punishment and suffering of Jesus began before the cross, but it is on the cross that he took the complete punishment for sin — that is, he died.

Verse 7 and the beginning of verse 8 describe what happened before the cross. Jesus did not open his mouth — that is, he did not say anything at his trial to defend himself. Why? Because he had made himself legally responsible for our guilt. He carried our sins to the cross, and on the cross he died for those sins: 'For the transgression of my people he was stricken' (verse 8).

In verse 10 we read: 'Yet it was the LORD's will to crush him and cause him to suffer' (NIV). This can also be translated: 'The LORD was pleased to crush him' (NASV), and means that God the Father took pleasure in crushing Jesus. Jesus was never more loved by his Father than when he was suffering on the cross — and yet, at the same time, it was the Father who was punishing him! God the Father poured out his anger against our sin on Jesus as our Substitute, but God's love rested on Jesus as his Son at the same time. For a time on the cross Jesus did not consciously experience the Father's love, and cried out, 'My God, my God, why have you forsaken me?' (Mark 15:34). He asks this question because he knows the Father loves him.

In verse 11 God the Father speaks, calling Jesus his 'righteous servant'. 'By his knowledge my righteous servant will justify many, and he will bear their iniquities.' Knowing Jesus, and knowing that he has taken our sin, is what justifies us.

The last verse of chapter 53 tells us that the cross is the reason God glorified Jesus: '*Therefore* I will give him a portion among the great ... *because* he poured out his life unto death.' The resurrection of Jesus and everything that followed it is Jesus' reward for what he did on the cross — he poured out his life to death, he was numbered with sinners, he bore the sin of many, and he made intercession for transgressors when he prayed on the cross, 'Father, forgive them, for they do not know what they are doing'(Luke 23:34). Then, as he died, he said 'It is finished' (John 19:30).

The words 'It is finished' are spoken by the Son of God himself, and he does not lie. If anything else is needed for us to be justified in addition to what Jesus has done on the cross, then his death is pointless. If any part of the work of salvation had not been completed, what hope would we have? But everything *has* been finished, and it is absolutely perfect. What does 'everything' mean? It means that all God's anger at our sin has been removed, that our sin has been taken away, that God's law has been fulfilled, that justification and righteousness are ours, that God promises to be our God for ever, and gives us his Holy Spirit. Everything has been done perfectly by Jesus. Nothing can be added to what he has done, or taken away from it — not by people, not by the devil, not even by God himself. Everything was done on the cross.

In reality this means that any sinner can go right now to the cross, and know that, because of what Jesus did there, he is forgiven, accepted by God and justified. Standing at the cross we receive all God's blessing. The cross says that God's anger against our sin has been exhausted, and righteousness has been provided for unrighteous people. At the cross we find rest from trying to please God ourselves. At the cross we see the greatness of God's love to us. At the cross we meet God and experience his amazing grace, and find peace with him.

God the Father gave us visible proof that Jesus completed everything; this proof is the resurrection. God raised Jesus from the dead to show that he agreed with Jesus' words 'It is finished!' The fact that Jesus ascended into heaven is further proof that his work was finished, and there was nothing more to do. This is made clear to us in the book of Hebrews, where we read that Jesus 'sat down at the right hand of God'(Heb. 10:12). The High Priest never sat down while he was serving in the temple; this was because his work was never finished — more sacrifices would always be needed. But Jesus, described in the book of Hebrews as our great High Priest, is sitting down in heaven. This shows us that his work is finished — there is no more need for sacrifices for sin.

These truths are full of encouragement for us. We can be sure that Jesus really did do everything, enough for even the worst sinner. If we think more about the completeness of what Jesus did on the cross, we will benefit in many ways: we will have a peaceful conscience; we will be able to deal with our doubts and unbelief; and we will grow in faith and confidence in our relationship with God.

We can experience different levels of rest, and as we understand more and more of the perfection of Jesus' work on the cross, we will experience more and more spiritual rest. We can have deeper peace in our hearts, too, and this is what the Holy Spirit gives us. How does he give us more peace? The answer is simple — by showing us more of what the cross means.

We will never get to the point where we don't need the cross. Even in heaven the cross will be central. In the book of Revelation, which gives us a vision of heaven, Jesus is frequently called 'the Lamb' (30 times). In John's vision he describes Jesus as 'a Lamb, looking as if it had been slain' (Rev. 5:6). Even in heaven, a place of absolute perfection, we will be reminded of the death of Jesus Christ. The cross will last for ever, and we will praise God for ever for what Jesus did on the cross, as we see in Revelation 5:9: 'They sang a new song: "You are worthy to take the scroll and to open its seals, *because you were slain, and with your blood you purchased men for God from every tribe and language and people and nation."'*

It is '*the Lamb*' who is worshipped by the elders (Rev. 5:6). The theme song in heaven is 'Worthy is *the Lamb*.' *The Lamb* opens the seals (Rev. 6:1); *the Lamb's* blood washes white (Rev. 7:14) and gives the victory (Rev. 12:11). The redeemed follow *the Lamb* (Rev. 14:4) and sing the song of *the Lamb* (Rev. 15:3). *The Lamb* fights and conquers (Rev.

17:14). The marriage of *the Lamb* is celebrated (Rev. 19:7). The church is *the Lamb's* wife (Rev. 21:9) and *the Lamb* is the light of the heavenly city (Rev. 21:23). These are just some of the references to Jesus as the Lamb in the book of Revelation. They show that the cross is central to the glory of heaven, and that in heaven we will have constant reminders of the cross. Just as a tree can never be separated from its roots, or a building from its foundation, so Christians will never become independent of the cross.

I cannot completely explain the place the cross will have in heaven; but what is clear is that the cross and the glory that we will experience because of the cross are closely connected. It would seem that we cannot enjoy the glory of heaven without remembering the cross. We will still rejoice in the cross of Jesus long after we have been made perfect. The cross is like the tree of life, which constantly produces all kinds of fruit (Rev. 22:2). Here on earth the message of the cross transforms lives; but is it not possible that in heaven the whole church will go on to become more and more beautiful, more and more glorious, as we appreciate more and more the greatness of the cross?

In Revelation 21:23 the Lamb is described as being the light of the heavenly city. 'The Lamb' is another way of saying 'Jesus Christ crucified', so it is the cross that lights up heaven. We will never be in a place where the sacrifice of Jesus has no meaning for us. The Lamb is the name used most often for Jesus in heaven. We worship him, obey him and honour him as the Lamb; we follow him now, and will follow him in heaven, as the Lamb. 'They follow the Lamb wherever he goes' (Rev. 14:4).

Chapter 5
Righteousness for unrighteous people

In the book of Genesis, chapter 15 verse 6, we read: 'Abram believed the LORD, and he credited it to him as righteousness.' This means that God credited, or gave, Abram righteousness, and treated him from that moment as if that righteousness was his own. Just like Abram (or Abraham, as he was later called), everyone who believes also receives righteousness from God. As a result, we can claim from God all the blessings that righteousness deserves.

God does not give us righteousness gradually, a little bit at a time, but he transfers it to us in one complete amount. We do not receive more righteousness if we have more faith, or more love for God, or if we pray more; we receive all of God's perfect, complete righteousness the moment we believe in Jesus.

This is God's way of rescuing sinners from the depths of their sin, and lifting them up, higher than even Adam was before he sinned. This crediting the believer with righteousness means far more than forgiveness and the opportunity to make a new start; we are now in a much more privileged position before God. It would be a great thing to have the same righteousness Adam had before he sinned, but we actually have something far greater! We have the righteousness of

Jesus Christ, the Son of God, the second and greater Adam. Just as Jesus is far greater than Adam, so his righteousness is far better than Adam's. This is the righteousness we receive from God, and can use to come before him.

This truth is so amazing, that it is not surprising to find some people who don't think it can be possible. Let me deal now with two main objections people have to this truth of Jesus' righteousness being credited to sinners. The first one is something like this: 'If I am not actually righteous, then how can God treat me as if I were? This is just pretending!' Such thinking shows that people have not really understood the subject. We need to see that God declares sinners to be righteous without compromising his own righteousness. God does not pretend that we are not sinners, or ignore the fact that we have broken his law. If he did, then he would not be righteous. Everything God does he does in a righteous, legal way. It is of course true that God saves us by his grace, but we must understand that God's grace is *righteous* grace; grace does not mean that God ignores our sin, but that he punishes that sin in Jesus.

When God the Judge declares a sinner to be 'not guilty', he does so without ignoring his law; he is a righteous Judge. God's love and his justice are not fighting with one another to see which is the stronger; God doesn't forgive us because his love is stronger than his justice. God loves to forgive sinners because he is love, but also because he is righteous. When a sinner comes to God to ask for his forgiveness, he can base this request not only on God's love, but just as much on God's righteousness. God forgives every sinner who comes to him because he loves to forgive, and because if he didn't he would not be righteous.

How can God be both forgiving and just? Because his solution to our sin depends upon what Jesus has done. God allows Jesus to be our legal representative, and to keep his law for us. This is a much greater solution than if God punished us for breaking his law; if he did that, his law would still be broken. In Jesus, we have God's law completely kept, while at the same time God can declare sinners righteous; everybody gains! God is honoured because his law is kept, and sinners receive forgiveness, and much more than that — the perfect righteousness of Jesus Christ.

This leads to the second main objection that people raise: that it is not right for God to treat people as having a righteousness they have not deserved. They think it unfair for people to benefit from what someone else has earned, without contributing anything themselves.

It is interesting to notice, however, that in everyday life there are many examples of people benefiting from something they haven't earned, and nobody objects to those! For example, nobody thinks it is unfair to inherit money or property from someone who has died. But this is exactly the same, only with material things instead of spiritual. One person freely receives something another person has worked for, and they do not complain about it — perhaps because we value material things much more highly than spiritual ones?

Another example in everyday life is that of a person who owes money. It is perfectly acceptable for someone else to pay the debt for him — even the law accepts this, and regards the man as being free of debt, even when it wasn't his money that was used to pay what he owed.

So people accept that there is nothing unfair about a person having their debts paid for by someone else, and that a person can inherit property or money someone else has worked for. So why do they say that this cannot happen in spiritual matters? If God is happy to have Jesus pay the debt we owe him, and to earn righteousness for us, why should we object? We are not the ones who have been sinned against!

The main reason people object to this is pride. We do not like to think that we are so spiritually poor that we can do nothing to save ourselves. We naturally want to earn our own salvation, and find it too humiliating to admit that we can't, and must receive it as a free gift. We think that, if we try hard enough, we can be righteous enough for God. We don't want to owe God anything.

The idea that Jesus had to live and die for us makes us feel so uncomfortable that we try to find other reasons for his life and death. One very popular theory is that Jesus' life and death are meant to give us an example of how we should live, and especially how we should react to suffering. If that is all the cross of Jesus means, then there is actually no hope left in this world. If all the cross shows is how to patiently suffer and die, then it also shows the victory of evil and Satan. If the best God can do for us is to show us a rare example of suffering and self-sacrifice, then we have to conclude that God has actually lost control of the world, and that sin has become too powerful for God to deal with. Jesus is just one more hero, who died for what he believed, but could not do anything to change the world.

On the other hand, if we accept that on the cross we have Jesus, the Son of God, dying in the place of sinners, then the cross becomes the central part of God's great plan to deal completely with sin and its effects, and to destroy Satan.

Chapter 6
How God's righteousness becomes ours

In the book of Jeremiah, chapter 23 verses 5-6, we have a prophecy about Jesus Christ; we are told that he will be called 'The LORD Our Righteousness'. Jesus himself was righteous — that is, he fully kept God's law, and was completely without sin. But we see more than that in this verse. He is described as being '*our* Righteousness', meaning that Jesus' righteousness is given to all who believe in him.

The moment we believe in Jesus, all our guilt passes over to him, and all his righteousness passes over to us. There are many verses that express this truth, such as Romans 1:17, Romans 3:22, Romans 4:5 and 2 Corinthians 5:21. This transfer of righteousness is complete and eternal; God now looks at us as having Jesus' righteousness, and treats us accordingly. We now have the right to everything that Jesus' righteousness deserves.

Let us think for a moment about the righteousness of Jesus Christ. Jesus was no ordinary man — he was a perfect man, and at the same time he was also God. So when we talk about the righteousness of Jesus, we are talking about a righteousness which is far better than any other righteousness. Even if you or I could live a righteous life (and we cannot), our righteousness would not come close to the righteousness of Jesus Christ.

Jesus *perfectly* loved God and his law, with the love of a perfect man and the love of God's own Son. There has never been another person who has loved God and honoured his law so completely. No one else has ever had such a perfect love for God and his law that he would become a willing sacrifice to pay for the law being broken. No one except Jesus has ever loved sinners so much that he would take the punishment for their sin, even to the point of dying for them. God's law had never been obeyed so completely as it was by Jesus, and God has never been loved more than he is by Jesus.

In Jesus, who is both God and man, we have a righteousness that can never be equalled. God the Father is delighted and completely satisfied with the righteousness of Jesus.

This is the righteousness we receive when we believe in Jesus; at that moment we become legal owners of the righteousness of Jesus, and from then on God treats us as if we are as righteous as Jesus.

What does this mean for us? It means that we can claim from God everything that Jesus deserves! It is wonderful to know that, covered in the righteousness of Jesus, we can come to God safely, but we can do even more than that — we can come and ask God for whatever we need.

It is like going shopping in a heavenly market; we buy everything we need and then pay using the unlimited credit of Jesus. What we can expect to receive from God depends on the quality of the righteousness we have to 'pay' with. If we try to use our own righteousness as currency with God, then we can't expect anything good, but if we have the perfect righteousness of Jesus, then we can ask for everything we need in Jesus' name, and God cannot refuse us.

To get this perfect righteousness all we need to do is agree with God's judgement that we are completely unrighteous, and ask for Jesus to be our representative. If we do not accept our need of Jesus, then we have to ask ourselves how far we think we can earn acceptance with God by our own efforts at keeping his law. It shouldn't take us long to realise that we won't get very far!

Anyone who simply comes to God and admits that they are unrighteous is certain to be welcomed. God is willing to receive anyone who comes like that; Jesus' righteousness is more than enough to cover all their sin, and to give them a new standing before God, which they could never have earned for themselves.

The more we think about the perfect righteousness of Jesus, the more we will have satisfied hearts and consciences. Our hearts will be satisfied because in Jesus we have found the only person who is truly worthy of all our love, and our consciences are free from guilt because we know that Jesus' righteousness is enough to cancel out all our sin.

The deepest peace in the Christian life comes from seeing that although we are still sinners, at the same time we are perfectly righteous in Jesus; that although in ourselves we are nothing, in Jesus we have everything; that although we are empty, in Jesus we are full; that although we are poor, in Jesus we are rich. The Christian who relies most completely on Jesus is also the holiest and happiest Christian.

Chapter 7
What is faith?

We have seen that the righteousness of Jesus becomes ours when we believe in him. The Bible is very clear on this, for example Romans 10:4 says: 'Christ is the end [or fulfilment] of the law, so that there may be *righteousness for everyone who believes.*'

So then, faith is very important. But what is faith? In this chapter we will look at what faith *is*, and what faith *is not*.

1. Faith is not righteousness

When the Bible talks about being saved 'by faith' this does not mean that faith is a good work that we do, as a result of which God justifies us. We are indeed saved by faith, but only because our faith connects us to Jesus Christ, and his righteousness.

Let us look at an example from the Old Testament. When the Israelites were bitten by poisonous snakes (Num. 21:4-9) and were dying, Moses was told by God to make a snake out of bronze and put it up on a pole. When anyone looked at the snake, he was saved from dying. In one sense we could say that the person was saved because he looked, but what actually saved him was looking *at the snake*.

In the same way, we are saved by believing *in Jesus*, not by our faith itself. Faith is not righteousness; it simply connects us to the righteousness of Jesus Christ, our Substitute.

2. Faith is not our saviour

We need to be clear about this: faith was not born in Bethlehem, faith did not die on the cross for us; faith did not love us, die to pay for our sins and faith did not rise from the dead. These are all things that our Saviour did, and because he did these things, we are saved.

3. Faith is not perfection

We have seen that God requires perfection from us, and that he has also provided that perfection for us, in Jesus. Nowhere does God require us to believe perfectly. This is good news, because none of us has perfect faith, so if God did require it, none of us would have any hope.

Because God doesn't demand perfect faith from us, we can have security and confidence. Our acceptance with God does not depend on how much faith we have, or how strong our faith is. No matter how weak or small our faith, if it is in Jesus, we have his perfect righteousness.

4. Faith is not payment for sin

Our faith does not in any way satisfy God's law, or take away any of the punishment our sin deserves. We need someone to do that for us. Our faith cannot pay for our sin, or wash us clean from it.

Faith brings us to the cross, where we see our sin paid for, and where we are washed clean. Faith is not something we do; faith accepts what Jesus did on the cross. Faith does not wash our sin away; faith takes us to the place where we are washed.

So what *is* faith?

1. Faith is receiving from God

We can understand faith in this way — faith is like the hand of a beggar, open and ready to receive. Or we can think of faith as a window; a window lets light into a room; it doesn't have any light of its own.

2. Faith is resting

Faith is the opposite of *doing* something to get God's forgiveness. Faith means giving up all the things we have been doing in the hope that God will love us and forgive us. Faith is agreeing with the truth that God does not wait for us to do good things before accepting us, and that he loves and forgives because he is gracious.

Faith stops relying on our own attempts to be good and somehow deserve God's blessing. Faith relies instead on the goodness of God, who sent his only Son for us.

3. Faith is seeing our need

Faith accepts that in ourselves we have nothing good to offer God, and that the cross is the only way we can come to God.

Faith saves us because faith means realising that we cannot contribute *anything* to our salvation. Salvation is *all* Jesus' work, from beginning to end. We are not saved partly by our faith and partly by Jesus. Faith doesn't believe in itself, but in the Son of God. Faith means understanding that you will always owe everything you have to the free love of God.

4. Faith is relying completely on God's mercy

This means coming to God simply as a sinner, without anything to recommend us to God. We come without excuses for our sin, without promising that we will do better in the future. We don't rely on anything we do, not even on our repentance, or on our prayers, or on our sorrow over our sin. It is not that these things are wrong, but we must not think that they 'help' God to forgive us. Faith realises that there is *nothing* we can do, and that we are saved only because of God's grace.

5. Faith leads us to the cross

By this I mean not only when we first become Christians, although that is true, but throughout our lives. At no time in our Christian lives do we stop needing the cross of Jesus; in fact, the secret of living a holy and happy life is to stay close to the cross, as we shall see in chapter 10.

By nature we all have a strong desire to justify ourselves; we easily become legalistic, and start to live as if we can please God by our own efforts. Faith, by leading us again to the cross, reminds us that only the death of Jesus saves us and only his righteousness makes us pleasing to God.

At the cross we see Jesus crucified for us. He is our righteousness, our peace and our strength, and we need him every day of our journey through this life.

Chapter 8
What the resurrection of Jesus means

Let us now look at the resurrection of Jesus, and what it means for us. Basically the resurrection is the visible proof that Jesus did everything necessary for us to be justified and accepted by God.

The Bible speaks about the 'power of his resurrection' (Phil. 3:10), and this does not mean that the resurrection has power to save us, but power to change us. Because Jesus rose from the dead, he is now able to work *in* us. Because Jesus is alive, we have a living relationship with him, and this living relationship is what develops holiness in us. However, all of this depends on what Jesus did *for* us on the cross. It is because of the cross that we receive God's forgiveness and are clothed in Jesus' righteousness; because of the cross we are justified and accepted by God.

Our salvation and acceptance with God depend on what Jesus did on the cross, and we must never forget that. All the same, the resurrection of Jesus is important, and we should not undervalue it.

The resurrection was an amazing event. People did everything they could to stop it, even putting guards at the tomb and a huge stone across the entrance. Even Jesus' own disciples, although they didn't try to stop the resurrection, didn't believe it could happen. They acted as people who have had all their hopes destroyed.

But what happens? The grave of Jesus becomes a place of light, not darkness, and of hope instead of despair. The angel comes and moves the stone; there is an earthquake (just as there was when Jesus died), and the guards were so terrified that they became 'like dead men' (Matt. 28:4). To the women, however, the angel says, 'Do not be afraid.' Why not? Because Jesus is alive. This is still the message for us today.

The angel gives the women the good news about Jesus' resurrection in this way: 'He is not here' (Matt. 28:6). Usually it was good news to say 'Jesus *is* here!' When Jesus was born in Bethlehem that was the good news, and when Jesus went around preaching the gospel and healing, wherever Jesus was, that was good news for people. Now the news that Jesus is not in the grave is wonderful news for us!

From this point onwards the disciples had a relationship with a risen Christ, and it is the same for us. When we believe in Jesus, we are connected to a risen Saviour and Lord. What does this mean for us?

1. We are secure

The life that Jesus had after his resurrection is a life that is stronger than death. This means that nothing can destroy this life. Believing in Jesus joins us to him, and we are described as being raised with him (Col. 3:1). We share in the indestructible life of the risen Christ.

2. We have power

After his resurrection, Jesus was given power over all things (Eph. 1:19-23). He showed this power when he rose from the dead, when he went up into heaven and sat down at the right hand of God the Father. One day he will come again with power. Right now Jesus is using this power to build his church, to save and to keep his people. This power is ours to use, whenever we are tempted or weak. It is his power that makes us strong.

3. We have encouragement

The resurrection does not mean that Jesus is now different from us. Of course it is true that Jesus is sinless, and we are sinners, but what I mean is, that after his resurrection Jesus was still completely human. The fact that Jesus rose from the dead did not change his humanity, or make him less able to identify with us; neither did it make it more difficult for us to know him. Actually, the opposite is true: Jesus is closer to us now, and even more able to sympathise with us.

This is a great encouragement to us in our daily lives. It also encourages us when we think about the future. The more we realise that we will die one day, the more precious it is to know that Jesus lives for ever, and we will rise to be with him.

4. We have joy

Jesus took our sins to the grave, and when he rose again, he left them there. He also left all his sorrows in the grave, and rose to a life of complete joy. We can read about this in many of the Psalms, for example Psalm 16:10-11. In verse 10 the resurrection of Jesus is prophesied: 'You will not abandon me to the grave, nor will you let your Holy One see decay.'

In the next verse we read: 'You will fill me with joy in your presence, with eternal pleasures at your right hand.'

After his resurrection Jesus experienced complete joy, in the way that only a risen person can. By faith we experience some of that joy now, in this life, but greater joy is waiting for us, when we will be with Christ for ever.

5. We have hope

1 Peter 1:3 says that we have 'a living hope through the resurrection of Jesus Christ from the dead'. What we have now as Christians is wonderful, but we have more to come — a kingdom, a city, an inheritance, a glory. All this belongs to us, and we know that we will receive it because Jesus rose from the dead and lives for ever.

We should think often about the resurrection of Jesus, because then we will be more conscious of the truth that we are risen with him. As we believe this, we will be more spiritually healthy, more holy, and more full of joy.

Thinking more about Jesus' resurrection also motivates us to share the gospel with others. The empty grave says to sinners, 'God accepted the work of Jesus as Substitute, and through him is forgiveness of sin, righteousness and peace with God.' The resurrection means that we are sure of our message; God is completely satisfied with the sacrifice of Jesus, and we can take the good news of forgiveness and righteousness to sinners everywhere — no restrictions, no conditions! We are equally sure that any sinner who comes to Jesus will immediately exchange life for death, freedom for slavery, joy for sorrow and certain hope for doubt and despair. Now that's truly good news!

Chapter 9
Being sure that we are justified

The message of the gospel is this: Jesus gave his life for us on the cross, and anyone who believes in him is forgiven and declared righteous. God has given us this message so that we may have eternal life, and also so that we may be *sure* that we have eternal life here and now. If we could not be sure about having eternal life, the gospel message would actually make us miserable — imagine knowing that forgiveness, peace with God, and eternal life are available, but not knowing if all that is mine; that's not really good news at all!

In this chapter we will look at two main differences between the teaching of the Reformation and the Roman Catholic Church on this subject, and then we will spend some time looking at why this is important for us today.

Firstly, the Reformers believed that **faith without works is enough to save a person,** or, in other words, we are justified by faith *alone* (for example, Romans 4:20). They believed that the Bible was very clear on this point, and we have already looked at this truth in earlier chapters.

What is the teaching of the Roman Catholic Church about justification by faith? It is different from that of the Reformers in two main ways:

1. How they understand the words 'by faith'.

If we look at how the Roman Catholic Church defines faith,

we will see that it is very different from how we defined it in chapter 7 of this book. The Roman Catholic Church accepts that a person is justified by faith, but only when that faith is accompanied by good works and other religious observances. They do not believe that a person is justified by faith *alone*, without works.

2. How a person is justified by God.

The Roman Catholic Church teaches the following: that before a person is justified they need to believe God's Word, turn to God's mercy and hope for his forgiveness; they also need to start loving God and hating sin, and begin a new life of keeping God's commandments. All of this is called 'preparation' for justification, and it shows that the Roman Catholic Church does not believe that someone is justified the moment they believe in Jesus.

Secondly, the Reformers believed that everyone who believes in Jesus **can and should be certain that he is forgiven**.

The Bible clearly tells us that salvation is a free gift, and that we can be sure we have it — for example, Acts 13:39, John 3:36. Nowhere in the Bible are we encouraged to doubt this; in fact the Bible never speaks of doubt as a good thing. It is true that Christians can sometimes doubt the fact that they are actually saved, but this is not a condition that God wants us to stay in. God wants every Christian to be confident that they are saved, and that being 'justified through faith, we *have* peace with God' (Rom. 5:1). The normal experience for a believer is to know that he is forgiven and has peace with God, and this knowledge is the foundation of his daily relationship with God.

What does the Roman Catholic Church teach on this second point? Basically this: that a person cannot be certain that he is saved. Their main reasons for saying this are:

1. Because no one is perfect, no one can be sure of God's acceptance.
2. If we could be sure, we would become proud. Not being sure that God accepts us keeps us humble.
3. It is possible for a person to become sure that he is saved, but only after living a very holy life and doing many good deeds. If he is holy enough, he may be acceptable to God.

Why does the Roman Catholic Church teach these things?

1. One reason is this: they do not want the power of the church to be weakened. If a person is sure that he is forgiven just by believing in Jesus, then he does not need a priest to hear his confession and declare him forgiven. If a person is sure that he is righteous because he has faith in Jesus, then he does not need the church to 'help' him get closer to heaven; he knows that Jesus has done it all already.
2. Another reason is simply this: we do not like to receive salvation just as a free gift, without contributing something ourselves. This is true of all of us, not just the Roman Catholic Church. By nature we are all deeply self-righteous, and we think that if we try hard enough we can be good enough for God; all we want is to have an opportunity to prove it.

So far we have looked at the Reformation teaching and the Roman Catholic Church teaching on the subject of being sure about our salvation. Let us now look at why this is important for us today.

1. *Knowing* that we are justified results in real peace

Consider these questions: How does God see me? Is he for me, or against me?

- If God is for me, then I have nothing to fear, now or ever (Rom. 8:31).
- If God is against me, then all I can do is be afraid.

But there is another possibility. If I am not sure whether God is for me or not, what then? This is such an important question that I want and need to have a clear answer. If I am not sure that God is for me, then I can have no rest in my soul. The only way I can have peace is if I *know* that I am God's, and he is mine.

Let me give you an illustration to help you see what I mean. Imagine that I have a child, and he is dangerously ill. How much can I concentrate on other things? Do I care what the weather is like, or what I eat, or if my business is doing well? Of course not! All that I can think about is 'Will my child live, or die?' I need to *know* that my child is out of danger before I can rest. It is just the same with spiritual things — I need to *know* that my soul is safe, and then I have peace.

2. *Knowing* that we are justified results in real holiness

We will look at this in more detail in our next chapter, but let me make this clear now. When a Christian knows that he is forgiven and God is at peace with him, he is truly happy, he enjoys his religion, and he becomes more and more satisfied with Jesus.

When we are not sure that God accepts us, this leads to us trying to show how good we are, so that God will be pleased with us. In other words, it leads to self-righteousness, and a life which is focused on ourselves and our good works; our good works become more important to us than the perfect life of Jesus, which was given for us.

So, ask yourself these questions: Am I satisfied with Jesus, and what he has done for me? If not, why not? Do I think that something needs to be added to what Jesus did on the cross? Isn't what Jesus did on the cross exactly what I need?

The cross shows clearly the free love of God to sinners; the cross takes away every barrier between me and God; the cross opens the way to me being welcomed by God, and receiving everything I need from him. If the cross does all this, then surely everyone who believes in Jesus can know that he is saved, and so can be free of all fear and guilt.

Chapter 10
Holiness

The apostle Paul says that we are declared righteous by God because we believe, not because we do anything (Rom. 4:5). Does this mean that good works are not important? Is Paul saying that Christians don't need to be holy?

No, definitely not. He is actually laying the foundation of good works, and taking away what stops us from being holy — unforgiven sin.

God wants us to understand the difference between faith and works, and to see which must come first. When Paul says that a person is 'justified by faith apart from observing the law' (Rom. 3:28), and that God credits righteousness to a person 'apart from works' (Rom. 4:6), he is not saying that good works are unimportant. He is making it clear that we do not *do* anything in order to be justified. Everything has already been done by Jesus, and faith connects us to his work.

When some of the Jews asked Jesus, 'What must we do to do the works God requires?' (John 6:28), Jesus gave them an unexpected answer: 'The work of God is this: *to believe* in the one he has sent.' Again, Jesus does not mean that good works are not important, but that we cannot make God pleased with us by doing good works. We are accepted by God when we believe in Jesus, and until this has happened we cannot actually do good works. Imagine a soldier who is in prison — he must be set free before he can fight. Or a runner, who has chains round his legs; he needs the chains removing before he can run. In the same way we need to be set free from sin before we can do good works.

We are justified *so that we may be holy.* But what is holiness? Our ideas of holiness are not the same as God's; we think that holiness can be produced by self-effort, and that fear of punishment can motivate us to be holy.

What God calls holiness can only be produced in conditions of freedom and peace with God. Forgiveness is essential, because only when we have experienced God's forgiving love will we want to obey him from the heart.

Real holiness is mainly about loving God, and we can't even begin to do that until we have found forgiveness with God, and have the confidence to come to him.

We have been bought by the blood of Jesus so that we may be new people. God has set us free so that we may be holy. God's free and unlimited love to us means that we don't serve him to get his approval, but because we are already accepted by him in Jesus.

God's love to us and our response of love to him work together to produce holiness in us. If we are afraid of God, or unsure of his love, we will not become truly holy. God's love is what changes our heart attitude so that we run in the path of his commands (Ps. 119:32).

Condemnation keeps us under the power of sin; forgiveness sets us free from condemnation. If we are in Jesus, God's law can no longer condemn us (Rom. 8:1-4). We move into the kingdom of love, and there we find both the strength and the desire to keep God's law.

51

When condemnation is taken away, our consciences are also set free from guilt. A guilty conscience makes us feel that we *must* obey God's law in order to avoid punishment, but it cannot give us the *desire* to obey. There is no pleasure in obedience that is motivated by a guilty conscience; we are only trying to be holy so that we won't feel guilty — not because holiness is desirable to us. Fear of punishment will never produce real holiness.

The free forgiveness of the cross is what deals with sin. In our hearts we are God's enemies, and only love can defeat this hostility. Our hearts will not be conquered by fear of punishment, and we will not begin to love God while we are still suspicious and afraid of him. The message 'God is love' changes our hearts. 'Perfect love drives out fear' (1 John 4:18). When we see God's love for us, we run into his arms; we hate everything that keeps us away from him; there is nothing we want more than to be like him, and share in his holiness.

What should we expect to see in the life of a person who is justified?

1. Peace

'Since we have been justified through faith, we have peace with God' (Rom. 5:1). Yes, we still have difficulties and problems, but God's peace encourages and comforts us. We are safe, and protected from evil.

2. Love

We owe everything to the love of God, so how can we not love him in return? Love produces love. 'We love because he first loved us' (1 John 4:19). The love of God to us produces love in us — love for God, love for other Christians and love for the world. God's love changes us; jealousy, anger and pride begin to die, and we become more gentle, kind, patient and humble people. How can we be proud and unloving when we have been so wonderfully loved by God?

3. Commitment

God committed himself to do everything necessary to save us, and we should be committed to him in return. The free forgiveness of God encourages and motivates us, making us brave and strong, giving us the energy to keep going, and guaranteeing our ultimate success. We are ready to serve with all that we have, because Jesus freely gave his life for us.

If sometimes we do think about giving up, the cross stops us. We have been crucified to the world; at the cross we were set free from the controlling power of sin, and we cannot go back to being the people we used to be.

4. Generosity

Our justification depends completely on the generosity of God. He 'did not spare his own Son, but gave him up for us all — how will he not also, along with him, graciously give us all things?' (Rom. 8:32).

God's gifts to us are priceless — he has given us his Son, his Spirit, eternal life and an eternal kingdom. Is it possible to receive such gifts from God and not become generous ourselves?

More than this, we are called to be self-denying people; even Jesus did not live to please himself (Rom. 15:3). It is a disgrace that Christians often live self-centred, selfish lives. 'Everyone looks out for his own interests, not those of Jesus Christ', Paul writes to the church at Philippi (Phil. 2:21). This has been a problem throughout the history of the church, largely because our hearts are so hard. As we believe in God's amazing love for us, we will be changed into people who love warmly, give generously, sympathise sincerely with others and help them unselfishly. We shouldn't think highly of ourselves for making sacrifices — after all, Jesus sacrificed himself for us!

5. Purpose

A justified person has good news to share, about how he has found righteousness and freedom and joy. He looks for every opportunity to share this good news, and to do good to others. He doesn't have any time to waste; he knows that his life now belongs to Jesus, who paid such a great price for him.

6. Full of praise and prayer

Justification has brought us into a relationship with God, and so we talk to him! We cannot be silent, for we have thousands of things to thank and praise him for, and thousands of things to ask him for.

7. Desire for change

God's forgiveness has brought us into a new world. We have new desires, and we see things in a new way. This means that we are not satisfied with the way things are. We want significant change, not just some political or scientific improvements. We want a better world, where Jesus will reign over all things. This is what we are looking forward to, and making every effort to be ready for. We believe the promise: 'He who is coming will come and will not delay' (Heb. 10:37), and so we wait in hope for him.

Holiness is about being changed, but we can change without becoming more holy. Many things in life change us, but they do not make us more holy. Time changes us; we change as we get older, but very often this change is just about getting rid of one sin or evil habit, only to replace it with another one. The influence of friends or society may change us, or the experiences we go through, but none of these actually change us on a deep level, in our heart.

The only power to change us at heart level is the cross. Only the blood of Jesus can cleanse us from sin. Jesus offered himself to God as the Holy One, so that his people might share in his holiness (John 17:19). Hebrews 10:14 says, 'By one sacrifice he [Jesus] has made perfect for ever those who are being made holy.' Our holiness is connected to, and comes from, the work Jesus finished on the cross. Hebrews 10:10 says, 'We have been made holy through the sacrifice of the body of Jesus Christ once for all.' In this verse we also see a connection between the death of Jesus and our holiness. The secret of a holy life is to constantly trust in the sacrifice of Jesus and rely on him every day.

The Bible never teaches that we can get to the point where we don't need the sacrifice and righteousness of Jesus. We will never, in this life, be without sin. If we think that we have reached that point, we are deceiving ourselves. Anyone who thinks that he is no longer a sinner needs to ask himself some serious questions: Do I never have even one wrong thought? Do I never lose my temper, or make a wrong judgement? Do I have no regrets about things I have done, or haven't done? Am I full of love to God and others every moment of every day?

We often want things to happen quickly, but God takes his time. In creation we see that the greatest trees grow slowest of all, and spiritual growth is often slow, too. God's purpose is that his people should be holy, but this does not mean that holiness will happen quickly. In fact the Bible speaks about a spiritual battle, and constant struggle with sin, which lasts until a Christian dies. So however slowly we are growing, we do not lower our standards or give up. We are aiming to become like Jesus.

Any progress in holiness that we make is only possible because we have been forgiven, and given new life by the Holy Spirit. Our lives should now be fruitful, and this fruitfulness grows out of our confidence that we have been accepted by God, and are loved by him. We are 'rooted and established in love' (Eph. 3:17), and it is this love of God that motivates us and makes us holy.

Part Two

The new life of the Christian

An updated and shortened version of three sermons on
Regeneration from 'The Christian Race and Other Sermons'
by J. C. Ryle, first published in 1900. The full work is
available from Charles Nolan Publishers.

Prepared by David Kingdon

Jesus said, 'I tell you the truth, no one can see the kingdom
of God unless he is born again' (John 3:3).

Chapter 1

The new birth — its necessity and its nature

We could demonstrate in many ways that the Bible is God's own Word. As a result it is altogether true and our only guide to heaven. Therefore it must surely be the duty of every thinking person to pay serious attention to every teaching that it contains.

One of the great teachings that stands out clearly when the Bible is fairly read is that every one of us must go through a spiritual change — a change of heart — sometime between the cradle and the grave. In other words, we must be born again. In the verse that forms our text, the Lord Jesus declares that without the new birth no one will see the kingdom of God.

Sinner, man or woman, boy or girl, notice that! There is no salvation without this new birth! Christ has done everything for us: he paid the price of our redemption, lived for us, rose again for us. But all this will do us no good unless there is this work in us: *we must be born again.*

In this chapter I shall try to show you from my text two things: *first*, the reason why we must all be born again; and *secondly*, what the expression to be 'born again' means.

The necessity of the new birth

First, then, why is this change of heart so necessary? The answer is short and simple. It is because of the natural sinfulness of every person's disposition. We are not born into the world with spotless, innocent minds, but with corrupt and wicked ones. We show our bias towards evil as soon as we have the power. The scriptural account is absolutely true — we are all sinful from birth and even conception (Ps. 51:5). In the beginning it was not so. Our first parents, Adam and Eve, were created holy, harmless, undefiled, without spot or stain or blemish. When God rested from his creative work on the seventh day, he declared them, like all his other works, to be very good (Gen. 1:31). But, sadly for us, Adam broke God's commandment and in consequence he lost communion with God. He forfeited the likeness of God in which he had been made. In short, he fell away from God and now we all, who are his descendants, come into being with a defiled and sinful nature. We are fallen and we have about us the marks of the old Adam. Should you doubt this, consider what we are by nature.

a) *By nature we are blind to Christ and spiritual reality.* People may be sharp and knowing in worldly matters, they may be wise in the things of time, but when they come to the Christian religion, their understanding seems blind; there is a thick veil over their hearts, and they see nothing as they ought to see. So long as they are in this natural state we may tell them about God's holiness and unchangeable justice but they are unmoved. The solemn realities of God's spiritual law and his judgement to come, of their own shortcomings

60

and their danger of destruction — all fall on deaf ears. They neither feel nor care about them and do not think seriously about them. They may hear these truths preached, but a few hours later they are no different to those who have never heard them. The precious truths of Christ crucified and his atonement for sinners, the wisdom and the excellence of the cross, are not appreciated at all. And why is this so? The Apostle Paul gives us the answer: 'The man without the Spirit does not accept the things that come from the Spirit of God, for they are foolishness to him, and he cannot understand them, because they are spiritually discerned' (1 Cor. 2:14). This is the real reason for all the weariness, lifelessness and carelessness which we often see amongst those who attend public worship. This is why there is so much terrible indifference about spiritual matters among rich and poor alike, and why the gospel appears to be a sealed book. This indifference comes from the heart. Some will always claim that they lack learning, or that they have no time, or that they have very special difficulties which no one else in the world has. But the truth lies far deeper. They *all* lack new hearts. If they had new natures, you would hear no more about learning, or time, or difficulty. Every mountain would be levelled, and every valley filled up, that the way of the Lord might be prepared (see Isa. 40:4-5).

b) *By nature we do not love the laws of Christ's spiritual kingdom.* We may not openly refuse to obey them, and we would be angry with any one who suggested that we have cast them aside, but we have no real delight in them. It is not our food and drink to do the Father's will (see John 4:34). By nature we love our own way and our own inclinations, and that is our only law. We devote ourselves to our own pleasure and our own profit, and we give no more than a few scraps of time to the one who made us and who has come to redeem us.

c) *By nature also we do not measure ourselves by God's standard*. What person ever takes the Sermon on the Mount (Matt. 5:1 - 7:49) as their rule of life? Who admires the poor in spirit, the mourners, the meek, those who hunger and thirst after righteousness, the merciful, the pure in heart, the peacemakers and those who are persecuted for righteousness' sake? These are all people whom the world despises. They are considered nothing when compared to people who are jovial and light-hearted, who love strong drink and sing lively songs. Yet it is these despised people whom Jesus calls blessed. What natural person judges sin in the way Jesus teaches us? How few look on drunkenness and fornication as damnable sins? Yet this is what the Bible says they are. How few consider anger without cause to be as bad as murder, and lustful looks as bad as adultery! — yet Jesus says they are (Matt. 5:27-28). Where are the people who strive to love their enemies, who bless those who hate them, and pray for those who persecute them? Yet this is the rule that Jesus has laid down. Why is all this? Surely there must be something radically wrong.

d) *The fact is that by nature we do not set ourselves to glorify God*. We take no pleasure in speaking to each other about him. The concerns of this world occupy a hundred times more of our thoughts, and there are very few groups of people in which mention of Christ and heaven would not bring conversation to a halt in an embarrassed silence! Why is all this? Some blame bad examples to explain their behaviour, others their poor education. But the evil is far more deeply seated: 'That which is born of the flesh is flesh' (John 3:6, Authorised Version). A change of nature is the only remedy. A corrupt tree can only bring forth corrupt fruit; the root of the mischief is the unrenewed heart of man.

e) *The truth is that by nature we are altogether unfit for Christ's kingdom in glory.* The lives we are in the habit of leading, the practices we love to indulge in, the tastes we are always seeking to satisfy, and the opinions we hold, all prove that we have no natural fitness for the inheritance that awaits the true Christian. The unrenewed person does not pursue holiness in every realm of life. Then what place can he or she expect to occupy in that blessed abode where 'nothing impure will ever enter it, nor will anyone who does what is shameful or deceitful' (Rev. 21:27)? How shall they stand in God's presence? They take no pleasure in prayer and praise on earth; how could they then enjoy the activities of that glorious dwelling where 'day and night they never stop saying: "Holy, holy, holy is the Lord God Almighty, who was, and is, and is to come"' (Rev. 4:8)? They do not count it a privilege to draw near to God through Jesus Christ, to walk with him, to seek close acquaintance with him. And where would be the comfort to them of dwelling for ever in the presence of the Lord God and the Lamb? They do not strive to walk in the steps of holy men and women of the past, they do not find inspiration in the example of the faith and endurance of the saints — so how could they join the company of just men and women made perfect? With what greeting, after a life spent in pleasing the devil and the world, would they salute Abraham and the Apostle Paul and all that blessed company who have fought the good fight? Alas! A natural man in heaven would be a miserable creature. There would be something in the air he could not breathe; the joys, the affections, the activities of heaven would all be wearisome to him. He would find himself unfitted for the company of the saints, as a beast is unfitted for the company of man; he would be interested in worldly and sinful things, but they would be spiritually minded — there would be nothing in common between them. I know that there are vain dreamers who fancy that death will work an alteration, that we may die sinners and rise again saints, but it is all a delusion. There is no such work of transformation in the grave. If we die spiritual we shall rise spiritual; if we die as worldly people we shall rise worldly. If we are to be made fit for heaven, our natural hearts must be changed *now* on earth.

f) *In short, the plain truth is that by nature men and women are all dead in trespasses and sins.* They have no hope and are without God in the world, in a state of miserable condemnation. And, worst of all, they neither know nor feel it. The cold corpse in the grave does not feel the worms that crawl over it; the sleeping wretch who has unwittingly drunk poison does not know that he will wake no more; and so also the unhappy man who is still unconverted cannot understand that he is in need of anything. Every natural man is dead while he lives — his body, soul and mind are all turned aside from their proper function, which is to glorify God. This is the state of every single soul at this minute, or else it used to be. There is no middle state. We cannot be half-way, neither dead nor alive. We were dead and have been brought to life, or we are now dead, and the work of new birth has yet to take place. This doctrine is not just for notoriously bad people like thieves or murderers: it is for all without exception. It touches high and low, rich and poor, learned and unlearned, old and young — all are by nature sinful and corrupt. It is because of this that Jesus solemnly tells us that unless we are born again we shall not enter into heaven. This may seem a hard saying, but it comes from the Lord himself. Search the Scriptures and you will see that it is true.

The nature of the new birth

Having demonstrated from the Bible the necessity of the new birth we must now examine what is meant by the strange expression 'to be born again'. It is a change through which we once more recover something of the divine nature, and are renewed in the image of God. It is a complete transformation of all the inner being. Its completeness and importance are most clearly shown by the remarkable picture that Jesus uses. He calls it a NEW BIRTH. We have all been born once as men or women, but we must all see to it that we are born again as true Christians. We have been born once as offspring of Adam; woe to us if we are not born the second time as offspring of God! We have been born of the flesh; we must also be born of the Spirit. We are born earthly; we must also be born heavenly. We are born corruptible, we must also be born incorruptible. Our natural birth is necessary for the life of the body. A spiritual birth is just as necessary for the life of the soul.

a) *To be born again is to enter upon a new existence.* It means having a new mind and a new heart, new views, new principles, new tastes, new affections, new likings and new dislikings, new fears, new joys, new sorrows, new love to things once hated, new hatred to things once loved, new thoughts of God and ourselves and the world and the life to come, and new thoughts about how that life is obtained. The one who has gone through the new birth is a new person, a new creation, for old things have gone away and new things have taken their place (see 2 Cor. 5:17). It is not so much that our natural powers and faculties are taken away and destroyed — I would rather say that they receive an utterly new bias and direction. It is not that the old metal is cast aside, but it is melted down and remoulded, and has a new stamp impressed upon it, and thus, so to speak, becomes a new coin.

This is no mere outward change, like that of Herod, who was impressed by John the Baptist (Mark 6:20), or of Ahab, who humbled himself and walked in sackcloth (1 Kings 21:27); neither of these had more than a temporary reformation. Nor is it merely a new name and new ideas, but the implanting of a new principle that will surely bear good fruit. It is the opening of the eyes of the blind and the unstopping of the ears of the deaf; it is loosing the tongue of the dumb, and giving hands and feet to the maimed and lame — for he that is born again no longer allows his members to be instruments and servants of unrighteousness. Instead, he gives them to God, and only then are they properly employed (Rom. 6:13).

b) *To be born again is to become a member of a new family — God's family — by adoption.* It is to feel that God is indeed our Father, and that we are made the very sons and daughters of the Almighty. It is to become citizens of a new state, to cast aside the bondage of Satan and live as free men in the glorious liberty of Christ's kingdom, showing our highest love to honour our King, and believing that he will keep us from all evil.

c) *To be born again is a spiritual resurrection.* It is only a faint likeness of the great change that is to come, but it is still a likeness, for the new birth is a passage from death to life (John 5:24). It is a passage from ignorance of God to a real knowledge of him, from slavish fear to childlike love, from sleepy carelessness about him to a fervent desire to please him, from lazy indifference about salvation to burning, earnest zeal. It is a passage from being strangers toward God to heartfelt confidence, from a state of enmity to a state of peace, from worldliness to holiness, from an earthly, sensual, man-pleasing state of mind to one of single-minded devotion to Christ Jesus. This is what it means to be born of the Spirit.

An appeal to conscience

It only remains for me now to urge this matter most solemnly on your consciences. If the new birth was a doctrine of secondary importance — one where a person may be left uncertain and still be saved, like church government or election — I would not press it on you so strongly, but it is one of the two great pillars of the gospel. On the one hand stands salvation by free grace for Christ's sake, but on the other stands renewal of the sinful heart by the Spirit. We must be changed as well as forgiven; we must be renewed as well as redeemed.

This matter is particularly urgent in these days. People may welcome sermons about Christ's willingness and power to save, and yet continue in their sins. They seem to forget that there must be the Spirit's work within us, as well as Christ's work for us — there must be something written on our hearts. The strong man, Satan, must be cast out of our house, and Jesus must take possession. And we must begin to live like saints on earth, or we shall never be numbered with them in heaven. Christ is indeed a full and sufficient entitlement to heaven, but we must show some fitness for that glorious dwelling.

I will not shrink from telling you that the doctrine of the new birth cuts every congregation in two; it is a line of separation between the good fish and the bad, the wheat and the tares. There is a natural part in every congregation, and there is a spiritual part. There are sadly few churches where we should not be constrained to cry, 'Lord, here are many called, but very few chosen.' The kingdom of God is no mere matter of lips and knees and outward service — it must be within a man, seated in the best place in the heart. I do not hesitate to say that there are many living members of churches who are exceedingly dead spiritually.

Examine yourself, I beg you, whether you are born again. Have you good solid reasons for thinking that you have put off the old self which is corrupt, and put on the 'new self, created to be like God in true righteousness and holiness' (Eph. 4:24)? Are you renewed in your mind? Are you bringing forth the fruits of the flesh or the fruits of the Spirit? Are your affections with the world or with God? Are you a natural person or a spiritual person? It would not be kind for me to keep back this vital truth, and it will not be wise for you to delay considering it.

Are you born again? Without the new birth there is no salvation! Without it you cannot see the kingdom of God. Consider how fearful it will be to be shut out of it, to see God's kingdom far away, like the rich man in the parable (Luke 16:19-31). How terrible to go down to the pit, well satisfied with your own spiritual condition, but still not born again. There are truly many roads to a lost eternity, but none so sad as that which is travelled by professing Christians — by men and women who have light and knowledge and warning and means and opportunity and yet go on smiling as if sermons and religion were not meant for them, or as if hell were a bed of roses, or as if God was a liar and would not keep his Word.

Are you born again? I do not want to fill your head, but to move your heart. It is not a matter of course that all who go to church shall be saved. Churches and pastors are meant to rouse you to self-enquiry, to awaken you to a sense of your condition. Next to that grand question, 'Have you taken Christ for your Saviour?' there comes another question, 'Are you born again?'

Dear reader, if you love life, search and discover your real spiritual condition. Suppose you find no evidences of new life: it is a thousand times better to know that *now* so that you may live, than to know it too late and to die eternally!

The new birth is a doctrine surrounded with gracious promises. No heart is too hard for the Holy Spirit to move. Many Christians could tell you of their past lives of terrible darkness that have now become light in the Lord. Many of the Corinthians were as bad as the worst of men and women, but Paul could write of them: 'You were washed, you were sanctified, you were justified in the name of the Lord Jesus

Christ and by the Spirit of our God' (1 Cor. 6:11). Many of the Ephesians were completely dead in sins as you may be at this moment, but God made them alive in Christ, and raised them up, and created them to do good works (Eph. 2:4-10). So examine yourself and draw near to God in prayer, and he will draw near to you. But if you do not ask for eternal life, you will not have it.

As for me, I pray that God, who can make all things new, may by his Spirit touch your heart with a deep sense of this truth. May you never rest until you are a new man or woman, and can say, 'I once was dead, but now I am alive; I once was blind but now I see.'

Chapter 2

The new birth — its cause, means and manner

In this chapter I shall set before you *firstly* the great cause of the new birth. Then I shall describe *secondly* the means, and *thirdly* the manner, in which it comes. I once more pray to God that this vital matter will not be carelessly put aside, but thought over and made useful to your soul.

The cause of the new birth

First, then, where does this new birth come from and how does it begin? Can any man give it to himself when he pleases? Can he change his own heart? No! That is impossible. We cannot give life to our souls any more than we can to our bodies. We cannot rise and become new persons in our own strength any more than we can wash away our sins by our own efforts. It is impossible! The natural man is as helpless as Lazarus was when he lay still and cold and motionless in the tomb (John 11:14,37-44). We may remove the stone (see verse 39), as it were, and expose the sad work of death, but we can do no more. A power far mightier than any power on earth must work before the natural man can awake and arise and come out as a new creation. To do all this is the special task of the Spirit of Christ, the Holy Spirit, whom Jesus promised to send (John 16:7-11). It is he who quickens; it is he who gives life. Only the Spirit can make the seed we scatter bear fruit. It is the Spirit who must move over these waste and barren souls of ours before they can become the garden of the Lord (see Isa. 58:11). It is the Spirit who must open the darkened windows of our conscience before the true light can shine into our hearts. And so, he that is born again is 'born, not of blood, nor of the will of the flesh, nor of the will of man, *but of God*' (John 1:13, Authorised Version).

This is a very humbling and awful truth. The conversion of a sinner can never be the light, casual matter that some think it to be. The great change that must happen within us can never happen by our own power. We cannot put off the old Adam like a coat, and put on the new man, just when and where we please. The new birth cannot possibly happen without the hand of God! Only the Power which first created heaven and earth, and called the fair world around us into being, can create new hearts in us and renew our minds.

You may dream of a deathbed repentance, and say to yourself that one day in the future you will become a Christian, but you don't know what you are saying. The softening of your hard heart and the living of a new life is not the easy matter that you seem to think. It is a work that can only be begun by God's power, and who knows whether perhaps you are putting it off too long?

It is not the plainest and clearest preaching, however fine it may sound, which can cause you to be born again. We may get Paul to plant and Apollos to water (1 Cor. 3:6) but the

Spirit alone can give the increase. We may gather a good-looking congregation with sinews, flesh and skin covering the dry bones (see Ezek. 37), but until the Spirit breathes upon them they are no better than dead. Not all the wisdom of Solomon, not all the faith of Abraham, not all the prophecies of Isaiah, not all the eloquence of the Apostles could convert a single soul without the operation of the Holy Spirit. '"Not by might nor by power, but by my Spirit," says the LORD Almighty' (Zech. 4:6). Therefore I call this an awful truth. I know the Spirit is promised to all who ask, but I tremble that you might delay and put off your soul's concerns for so long that the Spirit is grieved and you are left in your sins.

Yet although this truth may be awful to unconverted sinners, it is full of consolation to believers. It is full of sweet and unspeakable comfort to all who feel in themselves the holy workings of a new and spiritual nature. These can say with rejoicing, 'It is not our right hand nor our arm which has brought us on our way to Zion; the Lord himself was on our side. It was he who raised us from the death of sin to the life of righteousness, and surely he will never let us go. Once we were sleeping and dead in our trespasses, but the Spirit awakened us and opened our eyes. We caught a sight of the punishment prepared for the ungodly; we heard a voice saying, "Come unto me, and I will give you rest", and we could sleep no longer. And surely we may hope that he, who graciously began the work of grace, will also carry it forward; he laid the foundation, and he will not let it decay; he began, and he will bring his handiwork to perfection.'

The great cause and giver of the new birth is therefore very clear — it is the Holy Spirit.

The means of the new birth

Secondly, we must consider the means through which the new birth is usually conveyed. I do not wish to suggest that the Holy Spirit cannot work in extraordinary ways. Some have been born again without any outward and visible means having been used. For example, God promised through his angel that John the Baptist would be filled with the Holy Spirit even from birth (Luke 1:15). Yet it is plain from the teaching of Scripture that in bringing about the new birth the Holy Spirit usually uses means.

a) *The preaching of the gospel* usually has something to do with it when a man or woman is born again of the Spirit. This is a special means for turning people from darkness to light. Many can testify that it was through hearing sermons that they were first touched and brought to know the truth. It was Peter's preaching which first touched the people of Jerusalem on the day of Pentecost, so that 'they were cut to the heart and said to Peter and the other apostles, "Brothers, what shall we do?"' (Acts 2:37).

Before his ascension Jesus told his disciples 'repentance and forgiveness of sins will be preached in his name to all nations' (Luke 24:47). For the Apostle Paul, preaching took precedence even over baptising. 'Christ', he wrote, 'did not send me to baptise, but to preach the gospel — not with words of human wisdom, lest the cross of Christ be emptied of its power' (1 Cor. 1:17).

There is no means so blessed in the experience of Christ's Church as the plain preaching of the gospel. And there is no surer sign of decay and rottenness in a church as the neglect of preaching. There is no ordinance in which the Holy Spirit is so especially present as in preaching. It is through preaching that sinners are so often converted and brought back to God.

Since faith comes by hearing (Rom. 10:17), I must press upon you the importance of hearing Christ preached. Those who will not listen to the truth are the least likely to be born again.

b) Seldom, too, is a person born of the Spirit without *the Bible* having something to do in the work. The Bible was written by men who spoke as they were moved by the Holy Spirit (see 2 Peter 1:21). If you read it seriously and attentively you are seeking to know God in God's own way. You will find that among true Christians there are very few who will not tell you that the starting-point in their spiritual life was some saying or teaching in Scripture. Some part or portion of the Bible, pressed home upon their consciences by an unseen, secret power, was among the first things that stirred them up to think and examine their ways. Some plain statement of God's Word flashed upon their minds and made them say, 'If this is true, I shall certainly be lost.' Therefore I say to you over and over again, 'Search the Scriptures, search the Scriptures' (see John 5:39-40). They are the sword of the Spirit (Eph. 6:17). They are the weapon by which the devil is often driven out. So if you leave your Bible unread you are plainly not wanting to be born again.

c) Once again, men and women are not born of the Spirit without *prayer*. Either they prayed themselves, or someone has prayed for them: so Stephen died praying for his murderers

(Acts 7:60) and subsequently Saul was converted. The Lord loves to be sought by his guilty creatures, and those who will not ask the Holy Spirit to come down upon them have no right to expect any real change in themselves.

These then — the preaching of the gospel, reading of the Bible, and prayer — are the means God generally uses to bring about the new birth. I say generally, because it is not for me to set boundaries on the operations of God. I know that people may be spiritually awakened by illnesses and accidents, but I still repeat that preaching, the Bible and prayer are the channels through which the Spirit ordinarily works. I say further, that in all my life and reading I have never heard of a man who diligently, humbly, heartily and earnestly made use of these means, who did not sooner or later find within himself new habits and principles. I never heard of a man steadily persevering in their use who did not sooner or later feel that sin and he must part company — who did not, in short, become a real child of God, a new creature.

The manner of the new birth

Having considered the means through which the Holy Spirit generally brings about the new birth, we must now look, thirdly, at the particular manner in which this mighty spiritual change first touches a person. At the outset it is important to note there is a great variety in the ways in which the Holy Spirit works. We must never maintain that the Spirit is tied down to show himself in one particular way. We must never condemn a person and tell him that he is an unconverted sinner because his experience of the Spirit's working may happen to differ widely from our own.

a) *There is a great diversity in the time and age at which the Spirit works* that spiritual change that we call the new birth. A few have the grace of God in them from their infancy; they are, as it were, sanctified and filled with the Holy Spirit from their mother's womb. They cannot remember the time when they were without a deep sense of their own corruption and a real faith in Christ, and an earnest desire to live close to God. Such included Samuel (1 Sam. 1:28; 2:21), John the Baptist (Luke 1:15) and Timothy (2 Tim. 3:15). These people are really blessed! Their memories are not saddened by the recollection of years wasted in carelessness and sin; their minds are not defiled and stained with the remembrance of youthful wickedness. It is significant that many a believer could tell you that he or she got their first impressions of the Christian religion from the teaching and example of a father and mother who really feared God.

But many, perhaps the greater part of true Christians today, were not born of the Spirit until they had reached the years of maturity. These once walked after the course of this world. They may have openly served their lusts and various pleasures, or perhaps they were outwardly decent and yet regarded religion as a thing for Sundays and not as a concern of the heart. But, by some means or other, God stopped them in their tracks and turned their hearts to seek him, and they took up the cross of true discipleship. And bitter indeed is their repentance, and great is their amazement that they could have lived so long without knowing God. Yet how warm is the love they feel towards him who has so graciously forgiven them all iniquity.

There are some, some very few, who are first brought to God and born again when advanced in years. Yet it is fearful how few there are — a miniscule number in comparison with the multitudes who die in old age without ever seeking the Lord. This is not surprising when we consider how our habits become deeply rooted and therefore how hard it is for those who are accustomed to do evil to learn to do good. I know that with God nothing is impossible. I know that he can touch the rock that has long been unmoved, if he pleases, and make the water flow. But the fact is that we very seldom hear of old men or women being converted. As eternity looms over you, aged friend, now is the time when you should be seeking God.

b) *There is a great diversity in the ways by which the Spirit works* to bring about the new birth. Some are awakened suddenly, by mighty providences and interventions of God. They despise other warnings and then the Lord comes in and violently shakes them out of sleep, and plucks them like 'a burning stick snatched from the fire' (Zech. 3:2). Their awakening is often brought about by unexpected mercies, or by extraordinary troubles such as sicknesses or accidents that place a man in some great danger. I am certain that multitudes will tell us in heaven that their troubles did them much good: 'Before I was afflicted I went astray, but now I obey your word' (Ps. 119:67). This was the case with Paul: he was struck to the earth and blinded while on his way to Damascus to persecute the believers there (Acts 9:3-9). He rose from the ground a humbled and a wiser man. This was the case with the jailer at Philippi: he was aroused by an earthquake, and came and fell down saying, 'What must I do to be saved?' (Acts 16:26-30).

In contrast, some are awakened suddenly by very little and insignificant things. God often raises up Christ's kingdom in a man's heart by a seed so small and insignificant that all who see it are obliged to confess, 'The Lord has done this, and it is marvellous in our eyes' (Matt. 21:42, quoting Ps. 118:23). A single text of Scripture sometimes; a few lines in a book taken up by 'accident'; a chance expression or a word dropped in conversation, and never perhaps meant by him who spoke it to do so much. Each of these seeming trifles has been known to pierce men's hearts like an arrow, after sermons and ordinances have appeared completely ineffective.

Yet again, some are born of the Spirit gradually and insensibly. They hardly know at the time what is going on within them. They can hardly remember any particular circumstances relating to their conversion, but they do know this, that somehow or another they have undergone a great change. At one time they were careless about their spiritual state, but now they give it first place in their affections: once they were blind but now they see. This seems to have been the case with Lydia (Acts 16:14): the Lord gently opened her heart so that she responded to Paul's message. Here is one reason why we preachers sometimes hope and trust that many among the hearers in our congregations may yet prove children of God. We try to think that some of you feel more than you seem to do, and that the time is near when you will indeed come out and be separate, and not be ashamed to confess Christ before men.

c) *There is diversity in the feelings that the Spirit first stimulates*: each feeling is moved sooner or later, but they are not moved always in the same order. The new birth shows itself in some by causing great fear. They are filled with a strong sense of God's holiness, and they tremble because they have broken his law continually. Others begin with sorrow — they can never mourn enough over their past wickedness and ingratitude. Yet others begin with love — they are full of affection towards Christ who died for them, and no sacrifice seems too great to make for his sake. But all these feelings are brought about by the same Spirit; in this man he touches one string, and in that another, but sooner or later all are blended in harmony together, and when the new creation has fully taken place, fear and sorrow and love may all be found at once.

Concluding comments

I have tried in this chapter to show you that, although he works in various ways in different people, without the Spirit no one can be born again.

This, however, does not mean that you can wait lazily and idly, thinking that if the Lord gives you this blessed change, well and good, but if not, you cannot help it. The Lord does not deal with you as if you were machines or stones. He deals with you as those who can read and hear and pray. This is the way in which he wants you to seek him. Never was there a teaching so surrounded with promises and encouragements and invitations as this. Hear what Jeremiah says: 'I will put my law in their minds and write it on their hearts. I will be their God, and they will be my people' (Jer. 31:33). And again: 'I will give them a heart to know me, that

I am the LORD. They will be my people, and I will be their God' (24:7). And yet again, 'They will be my people, and I will be their God. I will give them singleness of heart and action, so that they will always fear me for their own good and the good of their children after them' (32:38-39). Notice also what Ezekiel says: 'I will give you a new heart and put a new spirit in you; I will remove from you your heart of stone and give you a heart of flesh. And I will put my Spirit in you and move you to follow my decrees and be careful to keep my laws' (Ezek. 36:26-27). Finally note what the Lord Jesus says: 'Ask and it will be given to you; seek and you will find ... For everyone who asks receives; he who seeks finds' (Matt. 7:7-8). 'If you then, though you are evil, know how to give good gifts to your children, how much more will your Father in heaven give the Holy Spirit to those who ask him!' (Luke 11:13).

This is what I want you to do — to ask, to pray for yourself with real earnestness. If any prayerless man shall say in the Day of Judgement, 'I could not come to Christ', the answer will be, 'You did not try.' Dear reader, be careful not to quench, grieve or resist the Spirit (1 Thess. 5:19; Eph. 4:30; Acts 7:51). God's grace has been purchased for you: strive and labour and pray that you may indeed receive it. God has promised that he will come down like rain on the dry ground — like water to wash away your soul's defilement, like fire to burn away the dross and filth of sin, and the hardest heart among you will become soft and willing as a young child.

Chapter 3
The new birth — its marks and its evidences

My aim in this chapter is to consider the marks or tests that you can use so that you can find out whether you have been born again. I shall set before you the character of those who are new creatures, and I shall warn you against certain common mistakes. Then I shall conclude the whole subject by appealing to your consciences.

Many take it for granted that they have been born again. They do not exactly know why, but it is something that they have never doubted. There are others who despise all such sifting inquiry — they are sure that they are on the right pathway, confident that they shall be saved. They may consider that if we talk about the marks of the new birth, we are sounding as if we are legalistic and believe in salvation by works. But, whatever men may say, you may be certain that Christ's people are different from the unconverted around them, not just in their talk but also in their life and conduct. They can be distinguished because there are evidences of God's renewing work by which it may always be known. Someone without any of these marks may well suspect that he or she is not yet on the right track.

But first of all I need to sound a note of caution. I do not want you to think that all the children of God feel the same way, or that these marks will be equally strong and plain in every case. The work of grace on a person's heart is gradual: first the blade, then the ear, and then the full corn in the ear. It is like yeast: the whole lump of dough does not rise all at once. It is as the birth of a baby into the world: first it feels, then moves and cries, and sees and hears and knows, and thinks and loves, and walks and talks and acts for itself. Each of these activities comes gradually, and in order; but we do not wait for all of them to appear before we say this is a living soul. Just so is it in every one that is born of the Spirit. He may not, at first, find in himself all the marks of the Spirit, but he has the seed of them all about him. Some he knows by experience, and all, in course of time, shall be known distinctly. But this at least you may be sure of: wherever there is no fruit of the Spirit (see Gal. 5:22-23), there is no work of the Spirit. 'And if any one does not have the Spirit of Christ, he does not belong to Christ' (Rom. 8:9).

Forsaking sin

First and foremost, forsaking sin is a mark of the new birth that John mentions in his first letter. He writes: 'No one who is born of God will continue to sin' (1 John 3:9). John is emphatic that 'No one who lives in him keeps on sinning. No one who continues to sin has either seen him or known him' (1 John 3:6).

Now I would not for one minute have you suppose that God's children are perfect. The Apostle John, in the same letter from which I have just quoted, declares: 'If we claim to be without sin, we deceive ourselves and the truth is not in us … If we claim we have not sinned, we make him out to be a liar and his word has no place in our lives' (1 John 1:8,10). It is clear, therefore, that we do not become sinless when we are born again. But it is equally clear that in the matter of breaking God's commandments, every one that is born again is a new person — a new creation (2 Cor. 5:17). He or she no longer takes a light and easy view of sin. They no longer judge it with the world's judgement. They no longer think that a little swearing, or a little Sabbath-breaking, or a little fornication, or a little covetousness are small and trifling matters. The born-again believer looks on every sort of sin against God or man as exceedingly abominable and damnable in the Lord's sight and, as far as in him lies, he hates and abhors it, and desires to be rid of it root and branch, with his whole heart and mind and soul and strength.

He who is born again has had the eyes of his understanding opened, and the Ten Commandments (Exod. 20:1-17) appear to him in an entirely new light. He feels amazed that he can have lived so long careless and indifferent about breaking them, and he looks back on the days gone by with shame and sorrow. As for his daily conduct, he allows in himself no known sin. He makes no compromise with his old habits and principles; he gives them up unsparingly though it cost him pain. The world may think him over-precise and a fool, but he is a new man, and will have nothing to do with the accursed thing called sin. I do not say that he never falls short, for he finds his old nature constantly opposing him — and this, too, when no eye can see it but his own. But then he mourns and repents bitterly over his own weakness. Yet he knows that he is at war with the devil and all his works, and strives constantly to be free.

Do you call that no real change? Look around you. Notice how people generally think very little about sin and, if they do, they do not take it as seriously as the Bible does. They suppose that the way to heaven is easy. Is not this mark of the new birth exceedingly rare? But for all this, God will not be mocked. People must know that until they are convinced of the awful guilt and power of sin and its awful consequences, and, being convinced, flee from sin and give it up, they are most certainly not born again.

Faith in Christ

The second mark to notice is faith in Christ. Here again I use the words of the Apostle John: 'Everyone who believes that Jesus is the Christ is born of God' (1 John 5:1).

I do not mean by this a general vague sort of belief that Jesus Christ once lived on earth and died — a sort of faith that even the demons possess (James 2:19). I mean, rather, that feeling which comes over a man when he is really convinced of his own guilt and unworthiness, and sees that Christ alone can be his Saviour; when he becomes convinced that he is on the way to being lost, and must have a righteousness better than his own, and joyfully embraces that righteousness which Jesus holds out to all who believe. He who has this faith discovers a fitness and a comfort in the doctrine of Christ crucified for sinners that he never knew before. He is no longer ashamed to admit that he is by nature poor and blind and naked, and to take Christ for his only hope of salvation.

Before a man is born of the Spirit there seems nothing especially appealing about the Redeemer (see Isa. 53:2), but after the new birth has taken place Jesus appears wonderfully attractive. Jesus is seen as the one worthy of the very highest honour who can relieve the greatest spiritual need and whose blood can wash away the foulest of sins. Before the new birth a man may show respect for Christ, and perhaps wonder at his miracles, but that is all. However, once born again a believer sees a fullness and a sufficiency in Christ for his salvation, so that he feels as if he could not meditate upon him enough. It is a most notable mark of a child of God to cast the burden of sin on Jesus, to glory in the cross on which he died, to keep continually in sight his blood, his righteousness, his intercession and his mediation, to go continually to him for peace and forgiveness and to depend entirely on him for full and free salvation. In brief, believers make Jesus to be the substance of their hopes of heaven — they live by faith in Christ, and in Christ their happiness is bound up.

It is the spiritual law of God which brings them to this. There was a time when they were ready to think well of themselves but the law strips off their miserable garments of self-righteousness, exposes their exceeding guilt and rottenness, cuts down to the ground their fancied notions of justification by their own works, and leads them to Christ as their only wisdom and redemption; and then, when Christ has truly become their Saviour, they begin to find that rest which before they had sought in vain.

These then are the first two marks of the Spirit's work — a deep conviction of sin and a forsaking of it, and a lively faith in Christ crucified as the only hope of forgiveness. These marks may well be unseen to the world, but without them no man or woman was ever made a new creature.

Holiness of life

The third mark of the new birth is holiness. Again the Apostle John makes this clear: 'Everyone who practises righteousness has been born of him' (1 John 2:29, ESV). The true children of God delight in making God's law their rule of life; it dwells in their minds, and is written upon their hearts — it is their meat and drink to do their Father's will. They know nothing of that spirit of bondage which false Christians complain of. It is their pleasure to glorify God with their bodies and souls. They hunger and thirst to have a similar attitude to that of their Lord (see Phil. 2:5-8). They do not rest content with sleepy wishing and hoping, but they strive to be holy in every part of life — in thought, in word and in deed. Their daily prayer is 'Lord, what will you have us to do?' and it is their daily grief and lamentation that they have come so short and are such unworthy servants (see Luke 17:10). Remember, then, that where there is no holiness of life there cannot be much work of the Spirit.

Spiritual-mindedness

The fourth mark of the Spirit is spiritual-mindedness. We learn this from Paul's words to the Colossians: 'Since, then, you have been raised with Christ, set your hearts on things above, where Christ is seated at the right hand of God. Set your minds on things above, not on earthly things' (Col. 3:1-2).

He who is born again thinks first about the things that are eternal; he no longer gives up the best of his heart to the concerns of this perishable world. He looks on earth as a place of pilgrimage; he looks on heaven as his home. Even as a child remembers with delight its absent parents, and hopes to be one day with them, so the Christian thinks of his God and longs for the day when he will stand permanently in his presence. He does not care for the pleasures and amusements of the world around him; he sets his mind not on the things of the flesh, but on what the Spirit desires (Rom. 8:5). He knows that he has 'an eternal house in heaven, not built by human hands' (2 Cor. 5:1) and he longs to be there. 'Lord,' he says, 'whom have I in heaven but you? And earth has nothing I desire besides you' (Ps. 73:25).

Victory over the world

The fifth mark of the new birth is victory over the world. Again John makes this plain: 'Everyone born of God overcomes the world. This is the victory that has overcome the world, even our faith' (1 John 5:4).

The natural man, who knows nothing of the new birth, is a wretched slave to the opinion of this world. He follows and approves what the world says is right, and what the world says is wrong he renounces and condemns. He does not want to appear different to his neighbours. He worries what people will say about him if he becomes more strict than them. This may be the natural man's concern, but the born-again believer is freed from all this. He is no longer led by the praise or the blame, the laughter or the frown of children of Adam like himself. He no longer thinks that the sort of religion followed by people he knows must necessarily be right. He no longer considers, 'What will the world say?' but, 'What does God command?' What a glorious change has come about when a man thinks nothing of the difficulty of confessing Christ before men, in the hope that Christ will confess him and own him before his Father in heaven (Matt. 10:32).

The fear of the world is a terrible snare. With multitudes, it far outweighs the fear of God. There are people who care more for the laughter of a company of friends than they would for the testimony of half the Bible. But from all this the spiritual man is free. He is no longer like a dead fish floating with the stream of earthly opinion. He is always pressing upwards, looking up to Jesus in spite of all the opposition he faces. He has overcome the world.

Meekness

Our Lord pronounced the meek blessed and promised that they would inherit the earth (Matt. 5:5). Meekness is what he had in view when he tells us that we must change and become like little children. Meekness, then, is the sixth mark of the new birth.

Pride is the besetting sin of all natural men, and it comes out in a hundred different ways. It was pride by which the angels fell and became devils (see Jude 6). It is pride that brings many sinners to hell. A man may know that he is in the wrong about true religion, but be too proud to bend his neck and act up to what he knows. Whenever I see a man spending his time criticising other churches, and talking about everyone's soul but his own, I always feel in my own mind, 'There is no work of the Spirit there.' But he who is born again is clothed with humility. He has a very child-like and contrite and broken spirit; he has a deep sense of his own weakness and sinfulness, and great fear of a fall. You never hear him professing confidence in himself and boasting of his own attainments. He is far more ready to doubt his own salvation altogether and call himself the 'worst of sinners' (1 Tim. 1:16). He has no time to find fault with others, or be a busybody about his neighbours — enough for him to keep up the conflict with his own deceitful heart. His own inbred corruption is his bitterest enemy. And it is just this humility and sense of weakness which makes God's children men and women of prayer. They feel their own needs and their danger, and they are constrained to go continually to him who has given them the Spirit of adoption (Rom. 8:15), crying 'Abba, Father, help us and deliver us from evil.'

Delight in the means of grace

The seventh mark of the new birth is a great delight in all the means of grace (those things God has provided so that Christians may grow in grace). In his first letter Peter says: 'like new born babies, crave pure spiritual milk, so that by it you may grow up in your salvation, now that you have tasted that the Lord is good' (1 Peter 2:2-3). David expresses such a delight in the means of grace when he says, 'Better is one day in your courts than a thousand elsewhere: I would rather be a doorkeeper in the house of my God than dwell in the tents of the wicked' (Ps. 84:10).

What a difference there is between nature and grace in this matter! The natural man often has a form of godliness: he does not neglect the outward observance of religion, but somehow or other the weather, or his health, or the distance, contrives to be a great hindrance to him, and far too often it happens that the hours he spends in church or over his Bible are the dullest in his life.

But when a man is born again, he begins to find a reality about the means of grace, which once he did not feel. The Lord's Day no longer seems a dull, wearisome day, in which he knows not how to spend his time profitably. Now he calls the Lord's Day a delight and a privilege, holy to the Lord and honourable. The difficulties which once kept him from God's house now seem to have vanished away: dinner and weather and the like never detain him at home, and he is no longer glad of an excuse not to go to public worship. Sermons appear a thousand times more interesting than they used to do; and he would no more be inattentive, or willingly go to sleep under them, than a prisoner would at his trial. And, above all, the Bible looks to him like a new book. Once it was very dry reading to his mind — perhaps it lay in a corner, dusty and seldom read — but now it is searched and examined as the very bread of life. Many texts and passages seem written just for his own case, and there are many days when he agrees with the psalmist, 'The law from your mouth is more precious to me than thousands of pieces of silver and gold' (Ps. 119:72).

Love towards others

The eighth and last mark of the new birth is love towards others. 'Everyone who loves has been born of God and knows

God. Whoever does not love does not know God, because God is love' (1 John 4:7-8).

He who is born of the Spirit loves his neighbour as himself. He does not share the selfishness, unkindness and ill will shown by the world. He loves his neighbour's property as his own: he would not injure it, nor stand by and see it injured. He loves his neighbour's person as his own, and he would count no effort wasted if he could help or assist him. He loves his neighbour's character as his own, and you will not hear him speak a word against it, or allow it to be blackened by falsehoods if he can defend it. He loves his neighbour's soul as his own, and he will not let him turn his back on God without appealing to him to stop. What a happy place the earth would be if there was more love! Oh that men would only believe that the gospel secures the greatest comfort in the present life, as well as in the life to come!

Concluding remarks

Such, then, are the marks by which the new birth in a man's soul may generally be discerned. I draw your particular attention to the first two marks: conviction and forsaking of sin, and faith in Christ. These are the marks on which each person must be his own judge. You must ask: 'Have I ever truly repented? Have I really closed with Christ and taken him for my only Saviour and Lord?' Let these questions be uppermost in your mind if you want to know whether you are born again or not. The last six marks — holiness, spiritual-mindedness, victory over the world, meekness, delight in the means of grace, and love to others, have this peculiarity about them, that a man's family and neighbours often see more clearly whether he has got them than he does himself. But they all flow out of the first two, and therefore I once more urge that you take especial notice of these two.

I want to conclude by addressing myself to the consciences of everyone, whether old or young, rich or poor, careless or thoughtful. I know that there is nothing popular or agreeable about the doctrine of the new birth. It strikes at the root of all compromising half-and-half religion, but still it is true. There are many who would like very much to escape the punishment of sin, but who will not strive to be free from its power. They wish to be justified, but not to be sanctified; they want to have God's favour, but care little for God's image and likeness. Their talk is of pardon, but not of purity. They think frequently about God's willingness to forgive, but little about his warning that we need to be renewed. But this is ignoring half the work that Christ died to perform. He died that we might become holy as well as happy. He purchased grace to sanctify as well as grace to redeem. Forgiveness of sin and change of heart must never be separated. 'What God has joined together, let man not separate' (Matt. 19:6). The foundation of God stands firm: 'If anyone does not have the Spirit of Christ, he does not belong to Christ' (Rom. 8:9).

It is easy to be natural men and women. We give no offence by being so. The devil tells us, as he told Eve, 'You will not surely die' (Gen. 3:4): but the devil is a liar and the father of lies (John 8:44). So long as we are natural men and women, we are dead already, so we must aspire to newness of life. Reader, what do you know of the workings of the

Spirit? I am not asking so much whether you can say which way he came into your hearts, but I do ask whether you can find any real marks of his presence in your life.

Don't be led away by false ideas. Head knowledge is not the new birth: a man may preach and work miracles and be an apostle like Judas Iscariot, yet never be born again. Church membership is not the new birth. Many sit in churches and chapels who shall have no seat in Christ's kingdom. They are not Israel who have the circumcision of the flesh outwardly. A man is really a Jew 'if he is one inwardly; and circumcision is circumcision of the heart, by the Spirit, not by the written code' (Rom. 2:29).

There were many Jews in New Testament times who said, 'We have Abraham as our father, and we have the temple among us and that is enough', but Jesus showed them that Abraham's children are those (and only those) who have the faith of Abraham and do Abraham's works. In a similar way, baptism is not the new birth either. To say that every person who has been baptised has been born again is contrary to Scripture and plain fact. Simon Magus was baptised but Peter told him later that his heart was not right before God (see Acts 8:20-23). Paul declared that though the multitude that left Egypt 'were all baptised into Moses in the cloud and in the sea … God was not pleased with most of them; their bodies were scattered over the desert' (1 Cor. 10:2,5). Peter also wrote that 'baptism … now saves you also — not the removal of dirt from the body but the pledge of a good conscience towards God' (1 Peter 3:21).

Please do not be led astray in this matter. Let nobody persuade you that someone who is a drunkard, a fornicator, a blasphemer or who is living simply for this world has been born of the Spirit simply because he or she has been baptised. If they do not have the marks of the new birth, they cannot have been born again. Remember, the outward seal is nothing without the inward work of God writing on the heart. To say that people who lack the marks of the new birth are born again is an unreasonable and unscriptural stretch of charity.

If you who read this little book have reason to think that you still lack the one thing needful, I beg you not to stifle your convictions or nip them in the bud. Do not go away like Cain and silence the voice of conscience (Gen. 4:8-9), nor dream like Felix that you will have a more convenient time than the present (Acts 24:25). There are two things that make a deathbed especially uncomfortable: first, purposes and promises not performed; and, second, convictions ignored and not improved. If you have any doubt that you have experienced the new birth, do not delay in coming to Christ. Press forward more and more to know Christ. And remember that it is a special mark of God's children that as they grow in age they also grow in grace, feel their sins more deeply, and love their Lord and Saviour more sincerely.